Contents

Special days.................................. 4

Spring festivals............................. 6

Weddings..................................... 8

Harvest festival..........................10

Christmas time............................12

Id ul-Fitr...................................14

Divali..16

Chinese New Year.......................18

Make it: Charoset..................... 20

Notes for adults.......................22

Index..24

Special days

4

Celebrations are special days...

Spring festivals

hop

Where would you look for Easter eggs?

6

These goodies are for an Iranian spring festival.

7

Weddings

bride

groom

This couple cut a cake at their wedding...

...and **this couple** share a **drink.**

9

Harvest festival

What would **you** take to a harvest festival?

10

Americans celebrate their harvest at Thanksgiving.

11

Christmas time

How would you decorate Christmas biscuits?

12

Yummy!

This Christmas bread looks a bit like a crown!

13

Id ul-Fitr

mosque

Muslims share a feast for Id...

14

dates

cheese-filled cakes

...and eat sweet treats.

15

Divali

Divali is the festival of lights.

16

Indian sweets

Hindus offer food in the temple.

17

People eat roast duck

at Chinese New Year...

...and give lucky

tangerines as presents.

19

Make it: Charoset

Mix these things together to make charoset.

grated apples ✓
dates and raisins ✓
apple juice ✓
cinnamon ✓

Mmmm!

This **treat** is **eaten** for Jewish Pesach.

21

Sparklers books are designed to support and extend the learning of young children. The **Food We Eat** titles won a Practical Pre-School Sliver Award, the **Body Moves** titles won a Practical Pre-School Gold Award and the **Out and About** titles won the 2009 Practical Pre-School Gold Overall Winner Award. The books' high-interest subjects link in to the Early Years Foundation Stage curriculum and beyond. Find out more about Early Years and reading with children from the National Literacy Trust (www.literacytrust.org.uk).

Themed titles
Celebration Food is one of four **Food We Eat** titles that explore food and meals from around the world. The other titles are:
Let's eat Breakfast   Let's eat Lunch   Let's eat Dinner

Areas of learning
Each **Food We Eat** title helps to support the following Foundation Stage areas of learning:
Personal, Social and Emotional Development
Communication, Language and Literacy
Mathematical Development
Knowledge and Understanding of the World
Creative Development

Reading together
When sharing this book with younger children, take time to explore the pictures together. Encourage children by asking them to find, identify, count or describe different objects. Point out different colours or textures.

Allow quiet spaces in your reading so that children can ask questions or repeat your words. Try pausing mid-sentence so children can predict the next word. This sort of participation develops early reading skills.

Follow the words with your finger as you read them aloud. The main text is in Infant Sassoon, a clear, friendly font specially designed for children learning to read and write. The labels and sound effects on the pages add fun, engage the reader and give children the opportunity to distinguish between different levels of communication. Where appropriate, labels, sound effects or main text may be presented in phonic spelling. Encourage children to imitate the sounds.

As you read the book, you can also take the opportunity to talk about the book itself with appropriate vocabulary, such as "page", "cover", "back", "front", "photograph", "label" and "page number".

You can also extend children's learning by using the books as a springboard for discussion and further activities. There are a few suggestions on the facing page.

Pages 4–5: Special days

Give each child an outline drawing of a fairy cake to decorate and cut out. Write on the name and birthday of the child. Position on a birthday calendar mural, with the cakes sorted into the right months.

Pages 6–7: Spring festivals

Mix crushed shredded wheat and melted chocolate and allow the children to shape the (cooled) mixture into nests to hold chicks or small chocolate eggs. Develop the theme of animal homes, for example through the song "Over in the meadow".

Pages 8–9: Weddings

Make a model bride and groom. Use clothes pegs for bodies, wool for hair, and fabric and tissue paper for clothes and flowers.

Pages 10–11: Harvest festival

Fill a basket with real fruits and vegetables for a harvest display. Taking turns, children can be blindfolded, take something from the basket, and then try to identify it by touch and smell.

Pages 12–13: Christmas time

Find out what children's favourite Christmas foods are, and compile a pictorial recipe book. Decorate its cover with a collage of Christmassy angels, bells, stars and holly leaves.

Pages 14–15: Id ul-Fitr

Id ul-Fitr marks the end of Ramadan, the Muslim month of fasting. Make hilal (crescent moon and star) decorations. Use gold foil for each star and silver foil for each moon. Use string to link them and for hanging.

Pages 16–17: Divali

At Divali, Hindus and Sikhs light up their homes and sometimes set off fireworks. Make firework pictures. Scribble all over paper in different coloured crayons, then cover with black crayon. Use fingernails or a coin to scratch away bits of black to create a colourful firework display.

Pages 18–19: Chinese New Year

In Chinese folk religion, each year is associated with an animal. Make cards for a pairs game, using pictures of the 12 animals: pig, rat, ox, tiger, rabbit, dragon, snake, horse, sheep, monkey, rooster and dog.

Pages 20–21: Make it: Charoset

Pesach celebrates the escape of the Jews from slavery in Egypt. Jews eat charoset to remember the building mortar used by slaves. Use cuboid and triangular blocks to build Egyptian-style flat-roofed homes and pyramids.

Index

a

apples **7**

b

birthdays **4–5**
biscuits **12**
bread **13**

c

cakes **4–5, 8, 15**
charoset **20–21**
Chinese New Year **18–19**

d

dates **15**
Divali **16–17**
duck **18**

e

Easter **6**
eggs **6, 7**

i

Id ul-Fitr **14, 15**

p

Pesach **21**

s

sweets **7, 17**

t

tangerines **19**
Thanksgiving **11**

w

weddings **8, 9**

Picture acknowledgements:
Alamy: 7 (Richard Levine), 9 (Photo Network), 10 (archivberlin/Fotoagentur/GmbH), 17 (ArkReligion.com); **Corbis:** 4–5 (Fabio Cardoso), 6 (© Ariel Skelley/Blend Images), 11 (Larry Williams), 12 (Ralf Hirschberger/dpa), 14 (Kazuyoshi Nomachi), 16 (Ken Seet), 19 (Franklin Lau); **Getty:** 8 (Ryan McVay/Stone); **iStockphoto:** cover balloons (Vasiliki Varvaki), cover tablecloth, 2–3, 13, 22–24 (Jon Helgason), cover, 13 (Andres Balcazar), cover sky, 22–24 (Judy Foldetta), 15 (Paul Cowan), 15 tablecloth (Gaffera); **Photolibrary:** 18 (Peter Brooks), 20–21 (Foodpix).